4-headed woman

poems

Opal Palmer Adisa

TIA CHUCHA PRESS

ACKNOWLEDGMENTS

Special thanks to Marilyn Nelson and Soul Mountain Retreat where the final touches of this manuscript occurred effortlessly.

Special thanks also to Devorah Major, Giovanni Singleton and Kevin Simmons, who saw many of these poems in first draft and offered keen suggestions.

Gratitude also to the ancestors and women all over the world.

Some of these poems were previously published in the following journals:
"Breaking Point I," & " Breaking Point VI," in Mosaic 23, Fall 2008
"Jaracatia," Alehouse, Number 3, 2008
"Loquat," "Back-Eyed Susan," Coconut Bread," "Corn-Bread," "Pita," "Crissa," "Cocoa Pod."
    Carambola," Rose-Hip," in Black Renaissance Noire, Volume 8/Issue 1, Winter/Spring 2008;
    Frontiers, Volume XVII, No. 3, 1996; Feminist Studies, Vol.21, No.1, Spring 1995; Feminist
    Studies, Vol. 20, No. 3, Fall 1994.

An earlier version of "Bathroom Graffiti Queen," was performed by writer at Afro Solo Theatre
    Company, San Francisco, August 14-17, 2003.
Current version was directed by Carla Blank and performed by Ayodele Nzinga at Timken
    Theatre, San Francisco, CA. March 14 &15, 2009 & Live Oak Theatre, Berkeley, CA
    March 26 & 27, 2009.
Current version was directed by Opal Palmer Adisa and performed by Ocean James at Dorsh
    Theatre, Frederiksted, St Croix, August 2012

Printed in the United States.

ISBN 978-1-882688-46-3

Book design: Jane Brunette
Cover art by Tamara Natalie Madden. Used with permission.
Back cover photo: Shola Adisa-Farrar

Published by: Distributed by:
Tía Chucha Press   Northwestern University Press
A Project of Tía Chucha's Centro Cultural, Inc.   Chicago Distribution Center
PO Box 328   11030 South Langley Avenue
San Fernando, CA 91341   Chicago, IL 60628
www.tiachucha.com

Tia Chucha Press is the publishing wing of Tia Chucha's Centro Cultural, Inc., a 501 (c) 3 nonprofit cor-
poration. Funding for Tia Chucha's Centro Cultural's programming and operations has come from the
California Arts Council, Los Angeles County Arts Commission, Los Angeles Department of Cultural Af-
fairs, The California Community Foundation, the Annenberg Foundation, the Weingart Foundation, Na-
tional Endowment for the Arts, National Association of Latino Arts and Culture, Ford Foundation,
MetLife, Southwest Airlines, the Andy Warhol Foundation for the Visual Arts, the Thrill Hill Foundation,
the Middleton Foundation, Center for Cultural Innovation, John Irvine Foundation, Not Just Us Founda-
tion, the Attias Family Foundation, and the Guacamole Fund, among others. Donations have also come
from Bruce Springsteen, John Densmore of The Doors, Jackson Browne, Lou Adler, Richard Foos, Gary
Stewart, Charles Wright, Adrienne Rich, Tom Hayden, Dave Marsh, Jack Kornfield, Jesus Trevino, David
Sandoval, Denise Chávez and John Randall of the Border Book Festival, Luis & Trini Rodríguez, and many
others.

for
Shola & Teju

Contents

PART 1 — WHAT'S INSIDE

PART 2 — THAT CERTAIN TIME OF THE MONTH

PART 3 — A CLEAR BREAKING POINT

PART 4 — GRAFITTI SERIES

what's inside

she chews and spits out

parts of herself

she cannot

integrate

Fry bread

after they   branded her
betrayer

she became
a vagabond

slinking behind
trees

jumping
over skeletons

every time she spat
a story got
lost

but for coyote
licking at her
phlegm

Injera

the other option
was to have eyes

in the back of her head
she was not into dictating

having learned the value
in flexibility

from living
more than four scores

she understood
some just had to be
led
even ordered
for the good

of the whole

faith was more than prayer

she was her own miracle

Roti

lizards crawled in front
of her path   paused

raised their necks tall
peered at her

she had a knack for figuring
out the finite in the infinite

she   the third child
breeched at birth

in her presence elders
hopped memory

of their yesteryears
often   folded in a drawer

firm with the knack
to enfold and transform

what she lacked in affection
she made up for

with a generous helping
of common sense

indisputable
the trump card

Coconut Bread

hungry chickens
in a coop

water spilling
from a busted pipe

the bass of the music
played a haunting rhythm

in her stomach
if this was how it had to be

she would recline
massage her lower abdomen

knead oil into her limbs
then go among them

a breeze they welcome
in the heat of the day

Corn Bread

exit backwards
her father warned

armor
against the covetous wagging

tongues of married
women

she who would not lay

beneath any man
or allow his insecurity

to determine the path
her feet would take

a smile can beguile
the most ruthless adversaries

she knows
the caterpillar's secret

Tortilla

walking barefoot
licking dew from leaves

her life was lived
outdoor among the
green stain of nature

she was never bothered
by the man everyone
said was mad

each day he came by
banging his cup and a bottle

sending the children and dogs
scampering   his voice a gong

but she offered him
coconut water then her palm

which he licked and sniffed
nodding off   suffused

from the blue garlic
of her breath

Pita

schooled in the art
of submission

she refrained
from wearing bright colors

or powdering her face
but in the bedroom

she would tease out
her hair

talk with the ghosts
who horded her stories

and laugh   laughed so hard
she fell to the floor

trembling in ecstasy
honey bursting from her pores

Pumpkin Fritters

two days before
the recital

she slipped
spraining her wrist

so she had to sit
out the concert

her   rival reaped
thunderous   applause

for the tune she had
practiced   so judiciously

worthiness was born
out of opportunity

maybe even selfless desire
or perhaps talent

brushing the tear
from her cheek

she learned
humility

Cocoa Pod

left to discover
her   predilection

she soothed
nocturnal dreams

crouching way up
in the tree

contemplating the distance
to the ground

she measured
herself

against the velocity
of the wind

falling was never
an option

too much salt
in her body to drown

Carambola

many nights she spent
gazing   at the stars

knew the world
was both   flat

and   round
she delighted in dancing

loved the grace
of her lissome body

pranced with the critters
and sang the promise

of sweet love
in the morning

.

Rose-Hip

a mountain
does not require

consensus
it needs

space   simple
or so it would seem

she knows the
price of creation

of course
most people aren't

interested
in being inventive

they vacillate between
being part of …

or criticizing
so she erected

a window
and planted a valley

from which to march
with time

Okra

nothing gave her
greater joy

than to knead
clay

mold it into something
she could never

have imagined
nzinga's warriors

something that feeds
people's hearts

stirred
their generosity

the blue cotton against
skin fortified their aim

amputated breasts
female archers

Bouquet of Herbs

the first time
she remembered

truly smelling

basil   oregano
chives and lavender

the tears rolled unchecked
down her cheeks

she was no older
than seven

she dreamed
of a memory

standing
in the kitchen

taking off the lid
of the pot

and finding a miniature
replica of herself

giggling unscathed
in the boiling water

that very day
she blended

the four herbs
and made a soup

her family
still refers to

as sweet
fingers

African Violet

perhaps
it was her father

who had insisted
on that specific color

lilac
for her dress

but daily
her mother demonstrated

what it meant
to be pedigree

there was never
any deviation

hard
as she   tried

to separate   herself
from them

everyone   knew her
even when she donned

a mask
they shouted

her   name

Black-Eyed Susan

never killed
even a fly

but someone
wanted to make

something of the fact
she wasn't able

to keep a boy-friend
her clothes

were often faded
her hair needed   conditioning

didn't seem to matter
dogs never walked
by her

without licking
her hand

or that words floated like bubbles

from her mouth
and her smile

was a kiss
that tickled

Loquat

the life she had been
living thus far

had been a see-saw
now she insisted on a   hammock

knew at the core
she was mainly sweet

though sometimes
the actions of others

caused her to forget   herself
get all tangy

she was doing well
better than well   truth be told

at long last
she had found   contentment

knew and appreciated
the varied roads that
led   home

Crissa

as a child she observed
cane-cutters sweating

under the sun   daily
always looking raggedy

their children running barefoot
their women buying food on credit

determined to end
the cycle

of those who seemed destined
to suck salt

she created a credit union
as an adult

established funds to help
workers buy homes

while still enjoying the sweetness
of the stalks

Atemoya

she listened
absent of the need

to offer her opinion
about what should

or should not be done
knew most people

need a good pillow
sprinkled with rosemary

on which to lay their heads
and ears to witness

their surrender
they usually did what

they wanted anyway
how more satisfying

when she massaged
the pain from one's body

then watch it float
moth like through the window

Gamboge

as she sits now
on the small   low bench

in her backyard
under the shade of the guinep tree

washing
her hands pause

as far back as she can remember
she has sat like this   even as an infant

near the gate of the school
beside her mother

who sold sweeties and fruits
to the children at lunch time

then as a woman
she sat like that

at the stall her husband
built for her to sell ground provision

if only she could stand up
and walk away

walk far off
without looking back

Bergamont

not knowing where it was going
but satisfying the urge

to go for a ride
go somewhere   unplanned

she jumped
on the bus   on impulse

as she ambled down the aisle
she glanced him

sitting alone
lost in his own thoughts

he was straight
from her dream

wafted in her father's
scent

Jaracatia

how then this aspiration
to be more than a spoke

in the wheel
but to be the wheel

and even the motion
that propels it forward

she believed
in the heat of the flame

knew there was water
to quench it

Pomello

the moon might be
unreachable

but laughter loitered
on every face

if there was no flour
she would use dirt

there would be bread
she didn't have to know

others did and knowing
was collective

generosity was being
a glowing planet daily

Soncaya

something about
being on her knees

the impossible possibility
of all that it means

turning over dirt
pulling weeds

pruning trees
planting seeds

the sedimentary familiar feel
of the compliant soil

on her fingers
the brown wet aroma

tomatoes will sprout
stretching sweetly crimson

as will eggplants
short but shiny mauve

elegant sun-flowers
and robust zinnias

the earth's
bounty

Umdoni

watching the constant
whirring of the windmills

she meditated
on her grandmother's photo

she wanted to know this ancestor
what they had in common

how the past
dove-tailed into the present

she cracked
the egg white in the glass

on good friday
what shape would her future take

Olosapa

she still kept
the stained panty

under her mattress
that first blood

reminder of her lost
innocence

not ready to trade
her tomboyish ways

for skirts and feet
crossed at the ankles

she spent all her free time
chasing dogs

while fathoming a way
to shed skin

into the moonless
night

Kabiki

adept at identifying
the stars

she was a disciple
of peace

cotton stuffed
in her nostrils

she created stories
while she worked

her face cloud white
the owl looking down from the tree

her son will never
fight their wars

2

that certain time of the month

she always popped the balloon

the crystal knitted

on her tongue

RED COUSIN

she is
here
again
every month
although i am never
sure when she
will appear

i feel myself

slowly losing it

i can't
prevent my crash
into the cotton tree

my fantasies are borderline
to be fondled roughly
urgently
by many hands
the owners of which i do not know
gender
irrelevant

to dig a hole and climb in

i blame
this red cousin
for my libidinous
cravings
antisocial undoing

oh to own my body
speak the language it understands
submit to shameful
desire
something in the mouth
a candy
a cock

drifting   too tired to stay alert
drifting   too tired
must get work done

she smells
this red cousin
ponderous as the earth
complete as yam
red cousin arrives
ooz
oozing

i have a date
i plea
i'm not up for your company

red cousin chuckles
lets herself in

we are attached

the comradery of sisterhood

PMS Advice Nurse

indulge red cousin
hers is but a short stay
four days tops
(in rare cases
seven days of hell)
cosset her
by pampering yourself
resist not
temptation of any kind
especially sweets
chocolate with brazilian nut
a must

Menses Recipe

4 down days
1 comfortable bed
tv with cable and remote
10 glasses alone time
3 tbs letting it all go
1 oz push on through

combine
alone time
letting it all go
push on through
in a bowl

mix gently with a plastic spatula
set it on the bed side table
turn on tv
demand pampering

CRAMPS

naked
spread-eagle
on my bed
i scan my brain
seeking to know
the texture of blood's memory
woven tight
fisting
in my uterus
is this about pleasures
once sown in the cavities of vessels
or of the hurts
let loose in its veins
what is
this blood

tender breasts
no delectation tonight
bloated stomach
a bestial beauty
back pain
fuck the world
cramps travel
from thighs to abdomen
vengeance unleash
my children are laughing
hot-water bottle
my lover has absconded
a cup of chamomile tea
friends whisper behind my back
dull echo pounding my head
the world keeps on keeping on
drip
drip
blood as unforgiving
as a noose
i am dead
weight

PMS Advice Nurse 2

before the onset of your period
get a manicure
you will be less likely
to commit murder
with pretty nails

only purchase
jump rope

Menses Recipe 2

3 cups   memory of the men who said you were beautiful
2 cups   perspective
1 cup   flash back to better times
10 tbs spoons   breath
a pinch   tears

mix memory and perspective together
let sit for 15 minutes
slowly pour in flash back
add breaths in between
cook for four days
glaze with tears

Corpus Luteum

the word menses was first used in popular english literature

if two or more

sometime before 1555   women

live in the same house

whenever the moon

is full

they will be united

by blood

please note

that house will not

necessarily be safe or friendly

emotions will be worn elastic

on the verge of fraying

unraveling

inevitable

low levels of

progesterone and estrogen

warning

warning

menses

catamenia

emmenia

period

i = feeling

unloved   erratic

no one takes me seriously

the internal dialogue

menses \men"ses\, plural noun.
latin expression mensis month,

plural menses months, the monthly courses of women

daughter #1

= overly dramatic

i have to do everything around here
disgruntled and pitiful
she rants at her siblings
i rant at her for ranting
we both need time-out
careening off the precipice
of the moon

p.s.
i don't know
why a rejected ovum
causes such self-depreciation
homicidal mediations
the need for
demonstrated   laudable
appreciations
love transformed
into a teeming
wasp's nest

about 50 millilitres of blood are lost during menstruation
once the corpus luteum dies
hormone levels fall
result the ejection of the endometrium
= menstruation

powerful women
truly
are to be
feared

main ingredients of most birth control pills
progestin and estrogen

PMS Advise Nurse 3

if you live in the house with another woman
it's worth considering
to agree
in advance
to avoid each other
when the moon
is full

positive energy
ignite sparks

give yourselves a break

allow each other space

Menses Recipe 3

fresh grown mint (any kind)
cayenne pepper
honey

bring water to boil
infuse mint
allow to seep for a few minutes

sprinkle in a dash of cayenne pepper
sweeten with honey

drink warm throughout the day

take steaming lavender bath

bask on clean silk sheets

PMS and PMDD Symptoms

anxiety
angry outbursts

bloating

cramps
cravings for salt & sweet

depression
decreased balance
dizziness

edema

fatigue

headaches

tearfulness

i
am
fine
i am fine
i am fine

iamfine
i am fine
really
fine

F I N E
FUCKED UP
IRRATIONAL
NEUROTIC
EMOTIONAL

just fine
thank you

my period again
the second time this month

most women have a 28 day cycle
i have a 21 day cycle
how special
it's amazing
i have enough blood
to do anything

1950 drs. gregory pincus and john rock
commissioned by
planned parenthood federation of america

goal develop simple and reliable form of contraception
worcester foundation for experimental biology
their lab
6,000 women in puerto rico and haiti
their guinea pigs
their invention enovid-10
marketed in the usa 1960

PMS Advice Nurse 4

make others step out of your path
take a leisurely walk on the beach
or near a body of water
in the absence of natural bodies of water
turn on your garden hose
create your own stream

practice speaking well below
your regular pitch level

Menses Recipe 4

1 bundle of callallo/spinach or greens
clove of garlic
yellow or sweet onion
thyme

wash greens thoroughly

sauté garlic, thyme & onion in olive oil
add greens
cook until tender (do not over-cook or as a flaccid penis)

even if you are a vegetarian
have lamb chops today

really you need to tear into flesh

drink a glass of merlot
with lunch and again at dinner

Starting Day

feces
digestive waste
expelled
from the anus
plural of the Latin word *fæx*
meaning "dregs"
shit
one of its colloquial

i feel like shit
actually worse
than poo

i understand shit
normally formed
diarrheatic
or constipated

how to name
what i cannot define
below the surface
of the water
but not drowned yet

feel like swearing
crying
need him to hold me
yet can't bear his touch
left alone
or entertained
moist groin
desire
a swinging pendulum

p.s.
blood is consuming
and consumes
jealousy
its alter ego

PMS Advice Nurse 5

do something silly: jump in a fountain
                     stick out your tongue at a police man
                     tickle your child until guffaw coughing

do sit ups
while contracting your stomach muscles.

repeat "fuck you" until your throat is parched

have a good laugh at your own expense

Menses Recipe 5

go to the acupuncturist
get needled and moxed
have your lover
massage your abdomen
engage in your wildest fantasy

It Will Run Its Course

9 p.m.
in bed
heat-pad on stomach
head a grid lock

be thankful
you didn't eat your children
today
be grateful
you didn't use your car to mow down
someone
today
be appreciative
you didn't slap the smirk
off anyone's face
today

1953
english doctor
katharina dalton
and colleague
dr raymond greene
coined the term
pms

you are not certifiable
it's not just
"in your head"
no need for
a lobotomy

PMS Advice Nurse 6

do handstands
jog in place for ten minutes
take vitamins   a

                      e
                      b3
                      b5
                      b6

check your   magnesium
                      chromium
                      zinc
                      calcium level

stay away from
anti
de
pressants

Menses Recipe 6

yield to temptation
sleep

yield to more temptation

intercourse is permissible
strongly encouraged
high libido

sleep some more

Contemplating The Next Step

i understand
why some mothers
leave
thursday would have been
the evening
three children
might have associated with
mommy gone
if i had not forgotten
how to run

the patriarch
still chides
don't tell me
it's that time of the month
again
feet chopped off
from behind
just above
the achilles heel

some proven remedies
skull cap
angelica root
st john wart
licorice root
black cohosh
chaste berry tree
milk thistle

despite symptoms
i perform
tapping on glass
the space between
flow and flash
will correct itself
bleeding is not
who i am
rather
how i show up
in adam's world

PMS Advice Nurse 7

sit in a lotus position
count the rhythm of your breathing

visualizing the blood
leaving you
gliding over rocks
polishing them
smoothly

smile
yes
you may giggle

blood free

Menses Recipe 7

vanilla and eucalyptus oil aroma therapy

gospel cd: mahalia jackson & yolanda adams

light a blue & white candle
(do not start a fire)

gossip if you must
(only about folks you detest)

affirm
i am woman
i love myself
perfect as i am

make it a mantra

Menstrual Hut

women go
to the hale pe'a
in hawaii
nourish their power
restore balance

jah-man
nu wan him woman
cook food
during dat time

stories whispered
nu eat stew peas
from any woman
yu can neva tell

it will bind
cast a spell
tie you to her
forever

simbu people
of papua new guinea
among indonesians
west africans
almost everywhere

sister-to-sister
relief from work
break from men
removed from the community
they told stories
guarded their solitude
grew powerful
influenced

                                        the men
                                using their blood
                    real   sometimes staged
                              to clear a space
                               for feminine
                                positioning

most times
i'm an even-tempered
congenial person
some even say
i'm gregarious
but not today

                               no private room
                         or isolated contentment
                                      give me
                                  shared space
                       where women-to-women
                                       gather
                            laugh at man's folly
                          and squash his fear

                             a menstrual hut
                      where women can just be
                                in charge of
                            nature' energy

# 3 a clear break ing point.

she spat out

a mouthful of teeth

pulverized fine

as grated corn

4-Headed Woman

somewhere
in the midst
of everything
buried between the garbage of roles
hidden among
the rubble of demands
is a headless life
probably my own

has anyone seen or
turned it into
the lost and found department

perhaps it was snatched
and gagged
by kidnappers
holding out for ransom

maybe
a pick-pocketer
grabbed it
assuming value

can do the mothering bit
but cannot do the wifing
poems must be written
who decides what's easier
what falls by the way

in my imagings
me was always
at the center
activities swirled
around me
not tornadic

me helter-skelter
clutching at air

this is my life
after all

Breaking Point I

the knife slips
severs muscles
finger hangs
attached by willowy tissue

an accident
cutting away thought
self erasure

diurnal stress
snaps the mind
a filament of meaning
loops until thread bare

the vulgar wound
discolored   swollen
draws loud sympathy

the mind
struggling for meaning
is met with
indignation

Breaking Point II

1
the birds no longer
sings by my window
everyone is over-worked
my boss shrugs
at my cluttered desk

i hunt for the telephone
among the pile of pink slips
from the receptionist
double check on the urgent
calls i must return
dogs are barking
with alarming vigor

every time i leave
my office cubicle
the chatter stops
their eyes follow me
like periscopes
but they all pretend
i am the none-descript
beige walls

2
call it premonition
i closed the blinds
after the second butterfly
flew into death
smeared on the glass

beware of friends
asking favors
they trample on your
exhaustion
swindle the little
time you are allotted
accuse you of selfishness

after you spend the greater
part of your weekend
listening attentively
trying to unravel their drama
you wonder how that big fly
got in circling the living-room
like a landing field
cough   again   cough
now chew on your palm

3
i listen to the news
eager to hear who
drove off the bay bridge
who jumped from
the golden gate bridge
who somersaulted
from the san mateo bridge
i am bridge for children
to husband to school
to survival
like a heron
diving is not my way
but i dip my head
and bring home food

negative energy
is out running me
the quiet i want to speak
is really a howl
wounded and abandoned

mommie is mean
i hate mommie
mommie is stupid
my children chant
i shut myself in the laundry room
slump on the floor
trash about
and gather my tears
in a cone

Breaking Point III

surely you see the dog
with wings flitting
through the grass

every time i smile
i hope no one
recognizes the dread
my eyes cannot shut out

but no one sees me
me self is
in
vi   si
ble

for the last two weeks
my head has been
the pounding of yam into fufu

a light stares out at me
whether my eyes are closed
or staring

i wake from sleep
every hour
certain
i have forgotten
to do something
very important
fold me self
pack me self
rest me self

although it's summer
the birds have not returned
every night
a dead chick
plops on my window still

BREAKING POINT IV

the ground swims
beneath me when
i walk

i am neither
miracle nor savior
so why the sea
has a hold of me
puzzling

very slowly
very quietly
i inquire
of myself

i advise myself
to listen
to myself
do as myself tells me
walk even though
running is more
logical

trap number 1
why haven't the other fishes
told their family
about nets lined
with worms

i won't listen
to myself
concentrating instead
carefully placing
one foot in front of the other

the fishes accuse me
my pace tricks the sea
to stay calm
the waves undulate
firing my jealousy

my ibo ancestors
drifted on the waves
all the way back to africa

did they stop to fish
when they were hungry
eat sushi and protect
their bodies with whale oil

i back-track
hoping to find
my
di vid ed
selves
solder me a boat

Breaking Point V

i cannot find words
that sound the laugh
i belch up

this laughter
lacks a larynx
if you heard it
you would know

all the animals
have jumped
ship

the night weeps
from such loneliness

i fell the hysteria
turning inside
on itself

i am not
rhetorical

the cow might
jump over the moon

but it was morning

Breaking Point VI

the slightest shift
of the wind
smarts my eyes

i do not measure
myself
neither by what
others say or do
nor by what they tell
me i should be

hold the light up
turn the light off

they do not want me
to be myself
want me to be
a bat folded in a cave
burnt toast
tossed to the chickens

i test ideas
with kaput words
not husband
children
or boss knows
my morse code
tapped out by the
humming bird

through neutered language
i find my way back
closer to the beginning
where unraveling began

the birds are returning
hear the water carried
on their wings

Breaking Point VII

i glanced at the african
shaped cloud
lopsided in the sky
too far away from itself
nothing is what it seems

i pace myself
willing the fatigue
to dissipate
as the river
nakeds itself
in august's drought

where does the smoke vanish
after the fire has cooled

my body hears
my head and responds
together they converse

long after
there is any evidence
of a blaze
fumes pollute the air
and so many stories
will never be written
or even be told

i am lost within
the loss of history

BREAKING POINT VIII

he took my tongue
that professor

the paramedic
pushed his hand
in my pants

my children are plucked
from my arms
who says who is crazy

he came down from the platform
from behind the podium
and asked me
the only black in the lecture hall
of over two hundred students
what's so special about black children

why did my tongue betray me
words ran from my mouth
crippled adults
escaping the blazing building

terror was a new feeling
i could not undress
their eyes echoed his scorn

whoever made me
a black woman in america
refusing the hand-me-down dress
i was ordered to wear

he clipped my tongue
the paramedics
strapped me in
the nurse admitted
me

Breaking Point IX

the train inside
my head never slows
every time
i nod off
it rumbles the ground
pitching me forward

i cannot get on the train
the man who sleeps
in the door way of the haberdashery
masturbates
the dog uses its paws
and covers its eyes

standing on the track
i try to stop the train
my arms waving
white flags on the battle field
bodies tossed   manure
i want to sleep not die

maureen weston
of peterborough, cambridgeshire
didn't sleep for 449 hours
14 days 13 hours
sat in a rocking chair

my body doesn't remember what
my hands want
in cairo i walked along
the banks of the nile
tracing a memory
i was a truant
twenty years missing

the train waits until late
to decide its destination
it's a run away train
get out my head
i implore
we argue about kendal crash
200 dead   700 injured
mass graves   body parts
never recovered
thieves stealing rings
watches   all the value
they can while blood
was still warm

stop the train
stop the train
i stay awake at night
insomnia my ally
sleep my enemy

every time
i lay my head on my pillow
the train races to the station
but it never gets there
scattered sand
during a desert storm

the train from beijing
to qingdao that killed
72 is still careening in me
my head

stop the train
stop the train

Breaking Point X

the moon weeps
softly in the bowl
of my cheek

the hen flaps her wings
gravity won't let her
ascend with the geese
yet they say i'm crazy

i who grow flowers
in my groin
praise the good
life i've enjoyed
not a shame
ascribed to secrecy

it was he who
spat at history
i couldn't own
in my face

he it was who caused
me to doubt the slender
stem atop the soil
joy its only defense

yes i ranted
all speed without breaks
i know now
the ground is there
even below the in-step
of my soles

Unnerving I

the wind flirts
with the flowers
but sometimes
just to make a point
it snaps one

she had smelled herself
long enough
to like her taste

when she had had enough
her fist smashed
through the mirror
and she licked the shards

seeing is often
akin to blindness

her blood dripped
into her open-beaked
mouth

Unnerving II

if "a" is the idea
then what is sanity

the knots in her stomach
alternated between granite
and success

she was going nowhere
had known it for a while
but lying to herself was a habit

the front of her dress was wet
tears she didn't have
vats of food stalked her
the queue of beggars
growing at her gate

did she make him
a monument to himself

she grated coconut
until her fingers bled

made an ebbo
wrapped her head

Unnerving III

she understood
that she did not understand

what they were talking about
any more than they understood

what they thought she had said
when she hadn't spoken

understanding
was not the problem

why tell the truth
if a lie adds more clarity

her heart was beating
yet she had not out-lived her time

someone was always
chasing someone

or their shadow
she didn't cut her eyes

or suck her teeth
she gasped

trying really hard
not to not lose it

the very idea was ludicrous
but she tried anyway

until her laughter
detonated

Break   Point.

pray
that you never live to witness
the tearing away
of tissue

      the grunt
that has no beginning
          but gets louder

pray
that she never reaches
the end of any rope
that blood doesn't cloud
her eyes

      run
when the sound
of a machete
hitting against a stone
sends sparks flashing

pray
she never forgets herself
completely
that she keeps love around
even in a bottom drawer

      hide
when the fist balls
knocking at thighs
it's not the sound
of talking drums

pray
despite scorn and rejection

despite faked food
or starvation

pray
pray hard and long

pray
as if your life depends on it
(it does)

pray
solemnly and diligently

that you never have
to witness
her
break   ing point

pray

keep
praying

pray

graffiti series

she's the fly

on the wall

she's talk

talking back

Public Restrooms Prelude

I
when i started elementary school
my mother showed me how to squat
over the toilet
public bathrooms are filthy
she said
you can catch germs

                    II
                    the school bathroom
                    was clean every morning
                    even after first recess
                    the rancid smell did not
                    assail your nostrils
                    but by lunch time
                    the floor swam in urine
                    i suppose everyone's mother
                    told her daughter to squat
                    but most got on the floor

                    i never drank after lunch
                    i had to hold it for 2 and1/2 hours

III
once while traveling
to the country on a mini bus
a woman sitting in the back hollered
to the driver
hold up driver   stop quick
me ahfi pee
the driver stopped the van.
i craned my neck and saw her squatting
by the side of the road
as she reentered the van

she said
tank yuh driver
me belly was almost gwane bust
a young man sitting beside me shook
his head knowingly and smiled
the journey continued

IV
when i was eight years old
while playing in the fields with
my friends i needed to pee
they sent me to squat near a tree
red ants swarmed my feet
large whelps covered my legs
and urine stained my ankles
the moral   look before you
squat to pee

V
when my grandmother caught me eating in
the bathroom
she slapped my hand
only nasty people eat in de bathroom
ah not training yu fah nastiness
 she said   kissing her teeth.

the bathroom was the only room in our house
that didn't have lizards
one night i spread a sheet in the bath tub
and slept there
my mother
frustrated with my phobia
pulled me awake
and marched me
back to bed

IV

in public restrooms
i never use my hand
to flush the toilet

i stay long in the stalls
that have writings
on the walls

Introduction to Graffiti

on the first day
of third grade
after lunch
when i went
into the toilet
the third stall
(like always)
i noticed
on the back of the clean door
written in pencil
so small it appeared
as a mark
i had to squint to read

pussy

i peed then reread
the word again
pussy

was someone speaking about
my private part
concealed between my legs
that place my mother
always made sure
i kept hidden

put your legs down
close your legs

don't climb that tree
without shorts

pull down your dress

my *chocho*

my little girl thing

                                   was someone looking
                                      under my dress
                                like those rude boys
                            crouching by the stairs

i ran my fingers
over the word
until it was erased

a black smudge
remained

Enticed by Graffiti

each day
i inspected the cubicles
to see which ones
had been baptized

written on the wall
behind the toilet
of the farthest cubicle
in block letters
in blue ink
P U   S
        S   Y
like an abstract painting
encircled in a heart-shape

a month later
the entire back door
was covered with
pussy PussY
in pen
pussy pussy
in crayon
my pussy
written in cursive
he sucked my pussy
sloppily scribbled
was she glancing around
as she wrote
PUSSY PUSSY
in large letters
he feels up my pussy
Pussy ugly pussy
in small neat script
not pussy
someone Xed out
but pumpum

my pumpum
written in even
elegant hand
and diagonally across
the wall in red ink

Pu S sy is dangerous
Pu S sy is sweet

Your Mama's pussy
P U S S Y

Inducted into the Graffiti Hall of Fame

i entered
the middle stall
freshly painted
took out the nail
from my pocket
and etched each letter
in my best penmanship

PUSSY
large and bold
then small and private
pussy

someone
would always
get under my dress

Bathroom Graffiti 1

before you send
your daughter off
to college
pay the exorbitant
tuition
buy her a
personal computer
and give her
a master card

insist
that she refrains
from using the
public restrooms

if by chance
she must
forbid her
to read any
of the scribbling
on the walls

no telling
what she might learn
or the ideas
she might ponder

Bathroom Graffiti II

if your daughter's
roommate
calls you up
and says
your daughter
refuses to
leave the restroom
that she visits it
daily
cutting classes
taking her laptop
into the stalls
staying in there
forever
sighing
singing
crying
scribbling frantically

don't hesitate
call the dean of students
at once
demand that
scrubbers and painters
be dispatched
to the restrooms
have all the walls
washed and laminated
call
the de-graffiti restroom counselor
immediately

your daughter
will need
all your support

total recovery
is almost always
impossible

Bathroom Graffiti III

your daughter
didn't take your advice
so what's new
you didn't listen
to your mother either

but you must tell her
you understand her obsession
confess your own
(past life) preoccupation
when you were
her age

you can picture her
furtive impatience
as daily
she dashes to the restroom
to inscribe
all her important
thoughts and questions
on the walls   of the cubicle

reading voraciously
making sure
to follow the advise
etched under her questions
being careful
not to flush   any comments

Bathroom Graffiti IV

in every cubicle
on every inch of wall
at my daughter's campus
in all manner of writing style
questions and answers abound

1. how often
do you masturbate?
and how long
does it take you
to reach an orgasm?

                2. i reach organism
                through masturbation
                but never while
                having sex

                                        3. what does it feel like
                                           is it incredible
                                        will i ever reach it
                                           please help

                4. have you discussed
                this with your lover
                   if not do so

                have your lover
                   him or her
                  please you
                 the same way
        you do during masturbation

5. try more foreplay
and by the time
you get around to intercourse
there shouldn't be
too much problem

6. not all women climax
during intercourse
see a sex therapist

7. if all of the above fails
try god
he gives good head

Bathroom Graffiti V

the concern
isn't always about
relationships
but most times
it is

                    i used to go out
                    with a nice man
                    but he dumped me
                    for a charming girl

                                        does that mean
                                        she wasn't charming
                                        or that he wasn't
                                        so nice after all

the word nice is
a 60's term that
shouldn't be applied
to humans
men and women
are good by nature
cars are nice
we are good

                        stay away
                    from charming men
                    nice men aren't
                        charming

                                        that's not true
                                        i met a nice
                                        and charming man
                                        yesterday
                                        but of course
                                        he was taken

you are wrong
emotions are not
nice or un-nice
they simply are
we (humans) are not
good or bad
our actions maybe
right or wrong
but that does not make
us good or bad people

most nice women and men
usually have hidden emotions
they are usually the ones
who kill their entire family
and the community
refers to them as "nice people
they wouldn't hurt a fly"
like the man who killed
his wife and three-year-old daughter
on the bay bridge
--ms Cynic

my advice to all
stay away from
nice people and refrain
from using the word
all together

Bathroom Graffiti VI

this cubicle
is for "serious" issues
with moral and political
implications

      power to women
      sister power
      girl power
      lesbian power
      dyke power

                              1. i'm pregnant
                            what should i do

                2. just get an abortion
                it's not as bad as
                people say

3. i had an abortion
and i haven't told anyone
well i guess i just did

      4. don't have an abortion
      put it up for adoption

             5.why should you bring
            a new life into the world
               only to give it up
                  to strangers
             you won't be able
           to guarantee its welfare
        and it will always wonder
          why its real mother
             didn't want it

6. every life deserves
to be born
think about your own life
what if your mother
had decided to abort you

7. birth involves a lot more
potential health complications
than abortion

8. *why go into a financial crisis*
to create a child who will have
hang ups about his/her real mother
in the future

9. *you can forget*
completing college
or your parents' financial support

10. life is precious
we should cherish it
you had one accident
don't have another

11. *if you're not white*
and have a child then give it up
for adoption
odds are it will grow up
in an orphanage or a series
of foster homes
p.s. i work my way through college
no trust fund here

12. yuppies want perfect
little blue-eyed babies
mormons want indian babies
to save their souls
from the fire of hells
no one wants black babies

13. prayer is the key
to unlock the door

14. you have options
remember

15. prayer didn't save jews
from the gas chambers
or blacks from 400 years
of slavery

Bathroom Graffiti VII

include in the
care package
you send your daughter
special de-focused
glasses
to be worn
always in the
restrooms
on her campus

these glasses
are guaranteed
to scramble
whatever
might be written
on the cubicles
in such places
they also cause
temporary
cramping in the joints
thereby
preventing your daughter
from the urge
to scribble
her latest
frustration

    think of
    this initial
    investment
    as insurance

      good luck

Bathroom Graffiti VIII

whenever you need
straight and direct responses
to your pressing questions
write them on the walls of the john

questions:

>   while having oral sex
>   with my boyfriend
>   he likes to lick my ass
>   although it feels great
>   i feel funny when i let him
>   what should i do

you will receive many responses

response 1
>   give him to me

>   response 2
>   *relax*
>   *sex is supposed to be fun*

>   response 3
>   >   don't let your boyfriend
>   >   lick your labia /clitoris
>   >   after your butt
>   >   or you may get a bacteria infection

>   >   >   but let him lick your ass
>   >   >   if it feels good

Bathroom Graffiti IX

it happens again
another sister
walking home late
from the library
was dragged in the bushes
and raped

men rape
men rape
is written in blood
all over the female john

                                        every woman
                                        who enters
                            sees the hand-writing on the wall
                            and tries not to think about rape
                            it's too intimate to far too many
                                but some sisters are angry
                                they want to feel free to walk
                            whenever   wherever they please

they respond in large letters
that go from ceiling to floor

rape is not
about sex

                rape is a crime of violence
                against women

castrate men
who rape

                castrated men
                can still rape

                                              testosterone
                                    is linked to violent tendency
                             removing the source of testosterone
                              may lessen the desire to cause pain

rape is terror

              the society does not value women

                      many women do no value
                      themselves

                                     no matter when or where
                                              it happens
                                      the woman will always
                                       be considered at fault
                               look at what she was wearing
                                          she knew him
                                          invited him
                                    she had no business
                                to be at his place that hour
                                      he's just a man
                                  you can't expect better

how far should women go
to stop rape

Bathroom Graffiti X

your daughter comes home
between spring break
you notice she has gained weight
and she seems obsessed with food
you invite her to go jogging with you
but she stares at you hard
then shaking her head sadly
begins to admonish you

> you should love your body
> and eat healthy for life
> don't try to be a 90 pound stick
> or go on crash diets

you look at her as if
she's lost her mind
she leaves you feeling stupid
and locks herself in the bathroom

confused
you pace around
five minutes pass
your daughter is still in the bathroom
ten minutes   twenty
concerned
you knock on the door
silence   then a flush
your daughter emerges with a grin on her face
you go to relieve yourself
then you see the scribble on the wall

<blockquote>

                 fat disempowers women
bullshit!   only if you think it does

</blockquote>

arrows connect both responses
you fight back tears
your poor daughter
stressed from the pressures of school
you go to wash your hands
and between the sink and the medicine chest
sprawled in red

diets disempower women
love your body

you wash the tears from your eyes
take a deep breath
and plan what to say to your daughter
but words leave you
the bathroom door reads

>   lack of self-esteem
>   disempowers women
>   it makes us
>   vulnerable to all kinds
>   of psychological manipulations

you nod your head in agreement
and enter the kitchen feeling
very thin

Bathroom Graffiti XI

my daughter claims
she gets more pertinent information
from the restroom walls
than in her political science class
she has concluded
women are at the forefront of social changes
when i press her on this issue
she invites me on a tour
of the 2nd floor women's room
at her campus

the moment i enter
i understand what my daughter has been telling me
slogans are everywhere

> *women*
> *if you're in an abusive relationship*
> *get out*

> *don't allow yourself to be seduced*
> *into submission*
> *control your own life*

we have zero tolerance for
sexism
racism
animal exploitation
homophobia

> *don't sit around complaining*
> *do something about it*

let politicians be accountable to you
your tax dollars pay the bastards

> *we're pissed*
> *we will fight back*

amazed
at the force and boldness of the statements
i decide to start a class in bathroom graffiti studies

Bathroom Graffiti Debate

In Three Voices (overlapping occurs)

V1: every semester
women work hard to decorate the walls
and every semester
they paint over them

                    V2: it's like they don't care
                    that we need this network

V3: we are not just
defacing the walls
for the fun of it
this is the most profound discourse
on campus

                    V2: the walls are like a magic slate
                    only we don't get to select
                    when everything gets erased

          V1: truth is relative
          find what you see as truth
          search your head and heart
          with all honesty
          study your eyes in the mirror
          be open to other ideas of truth
          but plead your case
          and live the way you want

V3: just don't hate others
it's stupid and idiotic

                    V2: don't let the capitalists rip off
                    your culture and sell it back to you
                    this university is a capitalist institution
                    that doesn't want to see women unite

V1: they give us women studies

V2: but they also give us
graffiti control workers

V3: figure it out
who has the power?
interrogate yourself

V1: who has more?
who does society favor?
who?

V2: women need a safe place
to be raw with themselves
to explore their feelings
without the scrutiny of men

V3: i want to love a woman
but never have before

V1: are you afraid to approach a woman?
are you a lesbian or a bi-sexual?

V2: there are lots of lesbians on campus
join the lesbian group
we meet every wednesday at noon

V3: female looking for a sweet femme woman
yes   i'm a butch
if you fit the description
email me at 2348tampon@yahoo.com
p.s. i like basketball
only ladies apply
sign   query

V1: sisters
please note
these walls are reserved
for serious questions
try the personal ads

i've had sex in this bathroom with a girl

2 girls want to join in

cool! let's set a date and time

let's not turn this sacred space
into a pick up joint
try to remember who we are
and what we are about

the globe needs more women
it's too male dominated
girl babies are still being killed
in too many places
throughout the world

we must help each other
men and women need to communicate
and learn to compromise

this guy made a crack to his friend
about he and i   going out
he made it seem like a joke
i overheard them talking
could this mean
he's actually interested in me
how can i find out?

you could try talking to him

but what if he doesn't like me
as much as i like him

then you know and can move on

if i were you
i wouldn't ask him
guys have a way of backing off
when a girl comes forward

      let me suggest that you make sure
      to cross his path regularly
      if he's interested
      even if he is shy
      he will ask you out

is it just me
or does anyone else worry
about being caught writing on these walls
does writing on it make you feel stupid?

              i don't care if someone sees me writing
              i get upset
              when no one responds
              or worse write something stupid

i hear you
i don't think everyone
appreciates the importance of this space

      i think some people are just
      playing around

but some of us
are serious

              no one has the right to hit anyone   right?
              it doesn't matter if she is a super bitch
              and he is a cocksucker

why is she a super bitch
a super bitch wouldn't let a man hit her
and why is a cocksucker with a woman

i think he hits her because
he's a closet queer
and is afraid of coming out

no one has the right to hit anyone
neither one has the right to hit the other
it doesn't matter if she is a super bitch
and he is a cocksucker.

hitting doesn't solve anything

neither does writing on walls
but we do it anyway

writing on the wall doesn't hurt anyone
and it mightn't help you
but it sure has helped me to figure things out

that's because you are brain dead

i think you're angry

right!
p.s.   i was   sexually abused

how does one forgive sexual abuse?
how can one forget and move on?

it's not healthy to try and forget
move on
we never really heal from sexual abuse
we never heal fully

forgiving can be an important part
of the process of healing
affirm that it wasn't your fault

forgiveness becomes not saying it's okay   for it's never okay
forgiveness becomes letting go of anger
to heal from abuse

        i recommend a good therapist
        or a non-judgmental friend

i recommend
the courage to heal

                        can you believe what
                        some people write on these walls?
                        where do they get this stuff from?

from their fears and dark secrets

hmmmm!

BATHROOM GRAFFITI QUEEN

A poetic performance piece

SETTING: A public restroom. The walls of the cubicle are made out of glass so that audience can see person using the toilet. There are three toilet stalls. Graffiti is written on the glass.

CAST
(This can be a one-woman performance but recommend two other actors.)

Bathroom Queen (BQ) – a woman in her mid forties to late fifties. She is eclectic. Dressed in one patterned stockings, her other leg is bare and toenails are painted in a variety of psychedelic colors. She is heavily made up. Her clothes are a mixture of African and standard American. She is an attractive woman, but there is an odd look about her. Her accent runs the gamut from African American vernacular to Caribbean to very British.

Female One – plays CHURCH WOMAN and WOMAN 2, ages 30 - 60

Female Two – plays GIRL, a teenager, and YOUNG WOMAN, in her 20s

----

Light comes up on Bathroom Queen (BQ,) sitting on the toilet, wiping herself. She flushes toilet and exits to sink. SHE speaks directly to the audience.

BQ
What you all looking at?
Your mama obviously didn't teach you manners.
Don't you know not to look at a woman when she's taking a piss?

(Introspective)
Inside the confines of the bathroom
her emotions spilled   neatly
pearl beads sown on a wedding gown

What kind of pervert are you anyway?
          (Pauses and looks around.)

You aren't a Graffiti Police are you?
          (BQ solicits response from audience.)
I'm asking: you ain't one of them Graffiti police are you? No. Good!

          (Introspective)
Forgetting was easier
than living with the loss
palatable as the sun heating zinc

          (BQ walks over to sink, washes her hands, and talks to herself.)

You know, I used to think there was no one worse than a meter-maid.
 I understand that folks got to eat and feed their children,
but imagine earning your living chasing after other people's car
who aren't breaking the law, just parking to take care of business.
I would have to starve before I take that kinda job.
Of course, I did apply for that kind of job and got it too.
But one day, was one day too much.

I knew … I mean I know that I am a queen so I walked off that job.
Left that little meter car parked right in the street, engine running.
          (Laughs.)
Damn! The things one do to make a living.

You've got to have principles.
Know what your limits are.
No matter how hungry or homeless you be. You've got to have ethics.
          *(Facing audience, BQ lifts up her dress, pulls her panties in place and
          straightens out her slip; she says aside.)*
I hate drawers. They sure ain't made for Black women's ass.

(Introspective)
Somewhere, somewhere in the middle
of the meaning of words
I was forgotten   dismissed
as summarily as the night

Now where was I.
   (SHE pauses/British accent)
I haven't had a fixed address for more years than I can remember.
I'm not homeless, nor am I a bum now, so don't go putting labels on me.
I have pride in myself. I haves standards.
I am a queen! An important and worthy queen! I'm Queen of Bathroom
Graffiti.
   (She fishes into her brassiere, takes out a marker and scribbles
   on the wall.)
What're you laughing at? *(Said defensively)*
Haven't said anything funny. What? You don't think I am a queen; well I am
more queenly than Queen Elizabeth herself. Aretha and I are on par. We be
some sure fine queens. Go on snickering. This isn't about you and I will not
be distracted from my royal mission.
   (Pauses/switches accent)
As I was saying. I be visiting all the lavatories – no, no no – hold up! What
the hell is a restroom?
Lord, don't get me started on the stupid names they be coming up for places.
Restroom my foot. The smell in this joint sure ain't inviting anyone to rest.
Anyway, as I was saying, I visit all the lavatories or water closets and respond
to the women's questions and make comments on what they be writing.
Women need a safe place to communicate.

   (Reflective)
high in the bosom of who we are
and who we try to be in the presence of others
lives a cactus   yellow
too much water   too much need
Sometimes, even if you have a best-friend there are things you want to ask,
but you're afraid because you don't want your friend to say you're stupid or
think less of you. So you go to a public lavatory and write your question
down. Then I come around and answer your questions.

(Speaking directly to 2 different women in audience, almost in her face)
Why are you acting like you don't know me. You are the one with all the
questions. I answered all your questions. Didn't I help you with the little prob-
lem with your husband? Girl, it's okay. Don't sweat it. I'll keep your secrets.
(To another woman)
I answered your question last week about masturbation, didn't I? I said go on
and do it, and if your man needs to watch you to get a hard on, let him.
Shoot! You're lucky he can still get it up.
(Back to entire audience)
Now, as I was saying before I got distracted. I used to think there was nothing
worse than a meter-maid, and if that's your job just go on like you don't hear
me. You know what's worse than a meter-maid? A Graffiti Police or Graffiti
Control worker. Now what kind of a job is that! Imagine spending money,
when so many folks are hungry and homeless, to pay others to go around try-
ing to catch some needy woman scribbling her message on the wall and eras-
ing it before I can answer that woman's question or worse, painting over my
answer before the woman can read it.
I am the Dear Abby of the bathroom. I am the restroom psychologist.
I am the president of the John. Whenever a woman has to urinate or defecate
or change her tampon or pad, she enters my queendom. Sometimes women
come in not having to do anything but write out their problems. They've gots
to write their problem. The John is the women's network.

    (Introspective)
inside   way deep inside
in the interior of the interior
under the shelf of learned perception
I live as woman with need and desire   inside

    (QB scrutinizes the graffiti on the walls as GIRL enters)

You see that girl there. See how she's looking around to see if anyone is
watching her. You know her – she's your daughter, your sister, your mentee,
your friend.
    (Tone shifts to melancholy; BQ speaks to herself)
She could be my baby, my Lotoya. Lotoya, the prettiest thing, if I say so myself.
Lotoya, baby where are you? Come to Mommy.
    (Reverts to regular tone)
I bet you that girl doesn't need to do neither number 1, 2 or 3.

Shhh. Shhh. Pay attention.   Quiet now and listen.

(GIRL, a 14-year old, looks at the mirror and primes, smiles at her
reflection, pushes out her chest. GIRL scans the stalls and seeing no feet,
enters one. GIRL doesn't appear to see QUEEN GRAFFITI who is
standing in the corner. GIRL talks as SHE writes)

GIRL

Help. I let this boy kiss me.
He French kissed me.
I also let him feel on my titties and put his fingers in me…
you know in my pussy. It felt good and I hecka like him, but I don't want him
to think I'm one of them easy girls. I ain't no slut.
What should I do? Should I let him continue to feel on me and stick his
fingers in my you know what?
P.S. I'm fourteen so don't tell my mom.

(GIRL glances at herself in the mirror before EXITING hurriedly.)

BQ

What I tell you?
She didn't need to use the bathroom, but she sure has a burning question.
        (Sighs)
My job ain't easy you know. I have to change up my handwriting.
I have to think about each person and what would be best for her.
Being a queen is not all that it's reported to be.
Now that child will be coming back tomorrow to see if anyone answered her
question. Sometimes, I wait to see what others say. Here comes "Miss Church
Lady."

(CHURCH WOMAN, a middle-aged woman ENTERS,
wearing very conservative clothes and a hat.
CHURCH WOMAN goes to stall where GIRL wrote.
CHURCH WOMAN hurriedly raises her skirt, pulls down her girdle,
her panty hose and her panties. Even before she is seated, she begins
to urinate.)

BQ

You can tell she been holding it a while. Poor thing almost wet herself. She is working on another yeast infection. Pussy needs air. Didn't her grandma tell her that. She has too much clothes on, then she wonders why she ain't had none for fifteen years.

Fifteen year! That's worse than being in jail. I guess she's been waiting on the Lord or Mr. Special. I suppose no one told her Mr. Special is a mirage. That pussy probably so funky from being locked up, if a man wanted some, once he got near, he would be turned off. Imagine wearing a girdle in this day and age. Everybody can see she's carrying a little weight; girdle don't hide that. And what's a little weight? A woman needs a little weight on her body to soften it out.

I feel sorry for her though. You can see in her face that's she's frustrated. Poor thing. Every woman who craves a man should have one at her disposal. I always keeps me two around, just in case one ain't available. Besides, a woman in her prime, such as me, needs more than one man. One man just can't keep up with a strong woman, and I'm a strong woman.

> (CHURCH WOMAN *wipes herself, and slowly pulls up her clothes as she begins to read what the girl wrote. She bends down and looks to see if anyone else is in the bathroom. Confident that she is alone, she reaches into her bag and pulls out her pen. A smile appears on her face.*)

CHURCH WOMAN

If it feels good, let him touch you. I wish I had someone to touch me. It's been so long I don't know what touching feels like. Sometimes it's all I can do to keep from screaming.

> (*She puts on a serious face.*)

You ought to be ashamed of yourself. You should never let anyone touch you unless you are married. And do not use that filthy P word.

> (CHURCH WOMAN *adopts a pious posture as SHE EXITS, with her head held straight. BQ chuckles then gets a worried look on her face.*)

BQ

Lotoya! That child loves to fool around. I can never keep up with her. Lotoya, baby, are you playing hide-and-go-seek again with Mommy?

That church woman is bipolar. Maybe she fooled you, but not me. I know her type.

See them all the time, wearing their two-sided faces, the same way they wear their clothes. Always pretending to love Jesus, but just as judgmental as you please, criticizing, thinking they are saved and the rest of us are sinners.

Well I ain't no sinner and I am always myself.

But this is the only place she can be herself, be honest about what she needs.

Of course, she would never admit her desire outside of this lavatory.

She's a good and decent woman. Everyone thinks she has it together.

But I know different. She's afraid to be herself and shatter her image.

Image is more important to her than her own needs.

Now she wasn't responding to that child's question. She's too focused on her own needs so I must give that girl a little perspective. I told you, my job isn't easy.

*(BQ reaches into her bosom and retrieves a marker.
BQ closes the door of the stall as SHE writes. BQ writes and thinks out loud.)*

BQ

I know how good it feels when someone you like pushes his fingers up your pussy, but what if he wants more and it feels so good, you can't stop him or yourself.

Are you ready to go all the way?

Are you prepared to insist that he wears one of them balloon things they call condom? Are you ready to have a baby if you go all the way and get pregnant?

I can't tell you what to do. Feelings are one thing and common sense is another. Sometimes they act like they don't know each other --more often they are complete strangers.

Does the boy like and respect you? Maybe that's the first question you should get the answer to.

Girl, with AIDS and other diseases blowing all over the place like breeze these days, sex can kill you.

(BQ EXITS STALL and again speaks directly to audience)

BQ

So what? You have better advice to offer her?

Advice is of no use to anyone, unless you take their feelings into consideration.

Besides, you know young people aren't gonna listen to you if you tell them to do this or that. You've got to let them make their own decision, or at least let them think they are. The most I can do is to give her something to think about so the fingers don't become a hard dick, robbing not only her virginity, but her possibilities.

> (ENTERS WOMAN 2- in her mid-thirties, wearing a tight-fitting dress.
> SHE goes into the same stall, pees squatting.
> WOMAN 2 reads the graffiti and reaches into her purse. She draws a
> line through what BQ wrote and writes below.)

WOMAN 2

If you don't want him to stick his fingers in you, send him to me.
I like young men.. Is your boyfriend cute?
He can do anything he wants with me. I am a liberated woman.
> (She starts to exit but changes her mind and returns and writes
> something else.)

WOMAN 2

Boys turn into men and men will break your heart.
(She opens door to exit, then changes her mind and returns in stall and writes)
P.S. If it feels good, it must be right so just go on and enjoy it; you only live once.
> (As she is exiting stall, she collides in BQ)
Woman 2: Look where you're going, you, you...
> (Woman 2 looks at BQ, stops and tries to move around her but BQ blocks
> her way.)

BQ

Who am I?
Yes me. Who am I?
I'm your mama, your sister, that girlfriend you abandoned for that last boyfriend who wasn't man enough to love you. Yes, it is me.
Your own self that you're looking at. That's who.

WOMAN

Please excuse me. *(Mumbles under her breath)*
Stinking old woman. Excuse me. I don't know you, nor do I want to.
(Woman 2 exits hurriedly)

BQ

Ignorance comes in all age and all levels of education.

See her. She's so locked up in that place when she was a teenager, she couldn't offer even a fool good advice. The nerve! Crossing out my wisdom and writing her fantasy. I ought to erase it, but I'm against censorship so I'm going to let it stay. We all need to hear things from many mouths so we can make the best decision for us.

(BQ paces)

Lotoya. Baby girl. Where are you? Are you hiding from Mommy again? You're my hope not yet baked.
You're my possibility not yet yawned.

(Back to audience)

Well it's getting late and I have to go. Do come back tomorrow evening and we'll talk some more. Before you go, make sure to write down your questions. I know you have many questions, but I just ask you to write one? If you want, you can make up one or ask a question for a friend. I'll be sure to answer them all. My ladies-in-waiting will give you paper and pens.

(BQ exits; stage goes dark. Paper and pens are passed to women in audience. A slide presentation of different bathrooms, or short video footage of women in various restrooms is shown while audience writes questions.)

(BQ Returns wearing a tiara. She has on a gown that's soiled and ripped. She has on one glove. She reenters stage dancing to instrumental jazz music.)

BQ

Oh that was a most splendid ball. I had the time of my life. Felt like Cinderella. Ooops! Seem to have lost one glove. I can't wait for Prince Charming to announce that he will marry the woman whose hand it fits. Oh do let me try. Let me try. See how dainty my hand is. I am sure the glove fits me. I lost it at the ball.

(BQ pulls off her shoe then tosses it and gloves on the floor)

What piece of crap is that! You expect me to believe that some handsome prince would go chasing after some dame he met at a ball because she fled at midnight and left her shoe behind.

Please! Give me a break!

If that was the only problem women have.

I can't find my child.

Don't know where my life is. And you are telling me a shoe or glove is going to solve my problems. Give me a break. I live in the damn lavatory. I dry clean myself as best as I can. Women and girls come in here and they don't even see me, or if they do, they frown and sniff their noses at me. Me. The Queen. I'm so tired, but here comes someone now.

(Young woman enters and goes directly to stall. She sits on toilet and writes.)

YOUNG WOMAN

I am nineteen. I broke up with my boyfriend, but he keeps stalking me. I am afraid of him. He says I'll always be his girl. What should I do? I can't sleep. I have ulcers. I am always looking over my shoulder.

(YOUNG WOMAN breathes deeply, then Exits stall. She stands in front of mirror and carefully, painstakingly applies make-up while BQ speaks.)

BQ

What can I say to this poor girl to put her mind at ease? I know what she means. Some man stalked me for five straight years. He was as crazy as a fly near fire, but no one would help me. The only way I got rid of him was to be more crazy that he was. It got to be that sometimes I had to leave a note to myself to remind myself that I should stop being crazy when I got home. *(Chuckles)* That's how crazy things can get trying to stay alive and safe.

(BQ pauses, reflects, pen in hand. After a while she begins speaking and writing.)

Honey, there's lots of crazy folks in this world, some more than others.

You can't let this man who's stalking you think you are afraid of him.

As long as he thinks that, he wins. Be brave.

File a police report although they probably will not do anything. Nada! Nothing! Damn hopeless the whole bunch.

Find some kind of spiritual practice that speaks to your soul.
Watch your back and get your brother or some male relative to beat that fool to a pulp.

>*(Young Woman smiles a knowing smile. She looks at herself and confirms her satisfaction with her appearance. She exits, glancing over her shoulder. BQ to audience)*

BQ

I don't want you to think I am a violent person. I hate violence, but medicine often tastes nasty. Some people need to hurt before they understand how their actions are harming others. I need you to hear me and understand. I am a believer in non-violence, but I will not wait to become anyone's victim, and I don't recommend it for others either.
(Pauses, to audience.) So please join me in holding that young woman in love and safety.

Lotoya…Lotoya, baby.
Lord please let her be safe.
Lotoya, baby… where are you?
Come to Mommy, please. Please come to Mommy.

>*(BQ walks to another stall and reads.)*

BQ

Here's a good question: "I'm a lesbian. I don't know how to tell my mother. Do you think she will disown me?" *(to Audience)*
See now. If she raised that question then she and her mother aren't close or she would know how her mother would respond.
I wish I had me a daughter. Well…I think I had a daughter, somewhere at one point, but I just can't remember.
(To audience) Do you have a daughter? *(BQ begins to write)*
Tell your mother and if she disown you, I'll be your mother.
>*(Tone Shifts)*
I had a daughter once. She was lithe and pretty.
She danced all day, danced all over the house.
We had a house. It was peach colored and we had trees too that I planted, apples and peaches.
I can't remember where my house is. I went for a walk one day, and when I returned the house was gone, my daughter was gone, even the trees were

gone.

(To audience) Do you know where my daughter is? Do you?
I don't care if she's a lesbian. I just want my daughter.

　　　　(Screaming)
I CAN'T FIND MY DAUGHTER.
HER FATHER TOOK HER.
WHERE IS MY HOME?
I LOST MY GLASS SLIPPERS.
Lotoya! Where is my glove?
I am not Cinderella. I am Cinderella.

　　　　(BQ begins to giggle then she tosses off her tiara.)
What the use of being a queen when they hire folks to paint over your words?
What's the use of being a queen when you have no daughter to be a princess?
What's the use?

　　　　(BQ goes in one of the stalls. Audience hears her blowing her nose.
　　　　In between blows, audience hears her reading and writing.)

BQ

Don't have the abortion.
Leave your husband even though he loves you.
Do I have a husband?

Wear the spaghetti dress to the party.
Lavender is your color.
Yellow was Latoya's favorite color

We must fight for everyone's freedom.
Yes, we must. I must look for my daughter and fight for her, for me, for us.

There are so many questions.
How can I answer them all?
You are right, Tampon is not safe, but I wear them sometimes.
We must protect the rain forest.
I have to protect Latoya.
I need protection, but from whom?

They ask me everything.
If you bathe daily, you don't need to douche.
The vagina is cleaner than the mouth.
What did he put in Latoya's mouth?

Right wing government upholds sexism and it's in my home;
it's everywhere like cracks in the sidewalk.
I hope Latoya don't break my back.

Questions and more questions.
don't the world understand women
are fighting for their lives.
We bleed every month.
Yes I get a craving for chocolate when I'm on my period, too.
But I drink raspberry tea instead.
Exercise daily and drink lots of water.
I could never get Latoya to drink water.
She was born with a sweet tooth.
       (BQ emerges dresses like she was in the beginning.)

BQ

Who you looking at?
Do you know me? Do I know you?
Have you asked me a question that I haven't answered?
I am Queen, Bathroom Queen, Graffiti Queen.
I visit all the water-closets and answer women's questions.
Men's too cause lot of folks who look like women are men
when they pull up their dresses. I knows it all.
I know the terror of ignorance and silence.
I know that women need to have space to write their fears and their questions.
I know we need to share with each other.
I am here for you and you and you.
I am here, Me Bathroom Queen.
I respond to everything you write.
Your questions will not go unanswered.

    (A recording of BQ humming is played under the remainder of the
    monologue, which SHE does while doing her nails. GIRL and WOMAN
    ENTER stage and pretend to write on the wall.)

BQ

Do you know my daughter? Have you seen her?

I was at the ball. The handsome prince will come with my glove to see if it fits my hand.

Ask your questions.

Don't be afraid to write. Don't let silence eat you to a wisp.

Turn your questions into blood spilled on the walls.

This is my kingdom. I am a queen.

A...

I am..

Am I queen?

A queen without a daughter.

A queen without a throne.

Latoya. Baby. Mommy believes you.

Mommy loves you.

Mommy will protect you.

Queen...Lotoya...

(Light fades slowly as BQ twirls around disorientedly.)